Forum On Animal Issues
With 25 Pet-Basics Thread Topics

Forum On Hypoallergenic Dogs, Pet Health Insurance Claims & Other Animal Issues

LA DI LA DAH

All rights reserved. No part of this book may be reproduced in any form or by any means without the prior written concent of the Publisher, excepting brief quotes used in reviews.

© 2010 La Di La Dah
Published by La Di La Dah, USA
Graphic design: La Di La Dah

ISBN-13: 978-0-9816629-7-8
ISBN-10: 0-9816629-7-8

TOPIC THREADS

1	Hypoallergenic and Non-Hypoallergenic Dogs	5
2	Breeds of Hypoallergenic Dogs	9
3	Are Portuguese Water Dogs Hypoallergenic?	13
4	Finding Hypoallergenic Dog Breeders	17
5	How to Care for Hypoallergenic Dogs	21
6	Grooming Tips for Dogs That Are Hypoallergenic	25
7	Special Needs of Hypoallergenic Dogs	29
8	Caring for Dogs with Hypoallergenic Reactions	33
9	Dog Health Insurance for Your Pet	37
10	A Comparison of Pet Health Insurance Plans	41
11	AKC Pet Health Insurance	44
12	Animal Health Insurance for your pet Ferret	48
13	Canada's Pet Health Concerns	52
14	Health Insurance for the Asian, Pet Pot-Bellied Pig	55
15	Comparison of Pet Health Insurance in Europe	59
16	Can Feral Cats Be Tamed?	62
17	Domestic Cat Breeds	65
18	Caring For Your Diabetic Cat	69
19	Cavy Care: Is A Guinea Pig Right For You	72
20	Dangerous Dog Treats	75
21	Fascinating and Novel Pets: The Turtle	78
22	Ferrets A Friendly Playful Pet	82
23	Hamsters Fuzzy Balls Of Fun	87
24	Thread 23: Helpful Hermit Crab Basics	91
25	Getting Your Pet Via An Animal Rescue Group	94

Thread 1: The difference between Hypoalergenic and Non-Hypoallergenic Dogs

If you have a child, who is susceptible to asthma and skin allergies, but who wants a pet more than anything, then a hypoallergenic dog might be the one solution for you. Dogs that are hypoallergenic may cause fewer allergic reactions in people who own them than other breeds. If you want to own a dog but can't be in the same room with one for long periods of time, you might be glad to learn this about hypoallergenic dogs. There are long hair, short hair, and hairless varieties of hypoallergenic dogs to choose from, depending on the particular allergies being dealt with.

Not long after the inauguration, media circuits excitedly announced the arrival of the Obamas "first" dog. The first family settled on a 6-month-old Portuguese Water Dog, which the Obama girls named Bo. The dog was a gift from Senator Edward M. Kennedy, who owned several Portuguese Water Dogs, himself. The President and first lady said their choice came down to a Portuguese Water Dog, because it was considered to be a good pet for children, who suffer from allergies.

Even though the differences between non- hypoallergenic dogs and hypoallergenic dogs may not be huge, they are apparently enough to reduce the amount and severity of allergy attacks (around certain breeds of dog.) While allergy attacks still might be experienced, the attacks will generally be less severe and less frequent. Dander is a collection of skin cells, dust, and other particles found in the air. Non-hypo-allergenic dogs tend to shed a lot. These dogs can also have an undercoat, a thick coat that protects them from harsh temperatures. This undercoat causes the dog to shed frequently and it can trap dander and other allergens in its fur. The fur can be loose and dense and contain a lot of dander as well. As the dog sheds, the particles of dander float around in the air and cause people to have allergy attacks.

Hypoallergenic dogs have shorter coats. The fur of these dogs is more like human hair, which means it will not shed as frequently as that of non-hypoallergenic dogs. Some breeds do not have an undercoat. Some hypoallergenic breeds, on the other hand, do not have hair at all. They are considered hairless even if they have hair on their paws and head. While this makes them unprepared for cold weather, they are perfect for people with allergies.

The fur of non-hypoallergenic dogs needs to be trimmed every few weeks in order to prevent it from growing too long.

Some non-hypoallergenic dog breeds may also salivate more often than other breeds, which can also cause a person's allergies to increase. While dogs cannot control the amount of saliva they expel, people allergic to dogs can have a difficult time when these dogs are present. Saliva contains bacteria that some people are allergic to.

Hypoallergenic dogs do not salivate as much as other breeds. This helps those who are allergic. This means that when the dog cleans itself, it will not leave as much bacteria behind.

People with dog allergies may also be allergic to dog urine as it too can contain certain kinds of bacteria. Urine from hypoallergenic dogs does not affect as many people either.

Tesco Pet Insurance   **Glossary**

A—C

Adrenal - small glands above the kidneys that produce hormones affecting the metabolism.

Alopecia - hair loss

Anaemia - a condition in which the oxygen-carrying haemoglobin pigment levels are below normal in the blood. Signs include pale gums and listlessness.

Bronchi - tiny air passages of the lungs that conduct air from the windpipe into the lungs and then into the blood stream.

Cage - a self-contained pet cage with a wipe-clean base that can be used as a safe sleeping area for your puppy. Available through pet stores in various sizes to suit different size breeds. Can also be used to transport dogs safely in cars when travelling.

Canine parainfluenza virus - causes flu-like symptoms and a high temperature of 30C/102F or more.

Cat shampoo - don't use a human shampoo on your cat as it could irritate her skin. Look for a specific feline product instead.

Cataract - the lens of the eye gradually becomes less transparent.

Colitis - inflammation of the bowel.

Thread 2: Breeds of Hypoallergenic Dogs

Hypoallergenic dogs might cause people to have fewer allergy attacks, possibly because their fur doesn't shed, they don't have an undercoat, or they don't shed a lot dead skin cells (dander).

There are, also, other qualities and considerations that can make certain breeds more appealing for your particular lifestyle. When looking for a hypoallergenic dog, you will have to decide on a breed of dog and also how the dog will fit into your lifestyle.

Popular breeds of dogs for people, who suffer from allergies, are: Irish Water Spaniel, Soft Coated Wheaten Terrier and Bedlington Terrier.

Many hypoallergenic dogs are small- or medium-size dogs. This means that they *require more attention than larger breeds*. Hypoallergenic dogs require more grooming than other breeds because they do not shed most of their hair; it just continues to grow. Learn as much as you can about grooming, brushing, and caring for your hypoallergenic dog. Their short coats need to be brushed a few times a week to prevent tangling. They will also need to be groomed every three or four months in order to maintain a healthy coat. Not grooming regularly will cause matting, which will have to be cut from the coat in order to prevent skin rashes and other problems.

For those who live in apartment buildings or small homes, a small dog is perfect. Smaller dogs are better for apartment living as they tend to bark less and require less room to move around in.

When looking for a hypoallergenic dog, it might also be helpful to research the following breeds: Maltese, Terriers, Schnauzer, Bishon Frise, Portuguese Water Dog, Greyhounds, and Irish Water Spaniel.

There are other breeds, but those mentioned are some of the more popular ones people buy and you might have fewer problems finding a breeder of them in your area.

If you own or rent a home, then a larger breed will be able to run around in the back yard. Large dogs are energetic and enjoy exercise.

Most breeds are very friendly and will live to be at least twelve years of age. These dogs enjoy companionship and exercise.

Thread 3: Are Portuguese Water Dogs Hypoallergenic?

Portuguese Water Dogs (PWD) are easy going and get along with most children and adults. If you are looking for a breed that does not shed and will fit in with your family, then the PWD is the breed for you.

Portuguese Water Dogs have short hair that doesn't shed and are considered to be working dogs, meaning they need to stay busy. While this breed is not as common as other breeds, if you want a dog that is hypoallergenic, lively, and enjoys companionship, then this might be the breed for you. Traditionally, PWD were used to assist in fishing expeditions, but now the Portuguese Water Dog is kept as a house pet. If you are considering buying a PWD, be prepared to have constant companionship. This breed needs to be walked and they need to be entertained throughout the day. If you need to travel on vacation or travel for work, you probably will have to board the dog so it won't be lonely.

Generally happy dogs, the PWD need to stay busy or they will get bored. When the PWD get bored or lonely, they will chew on anything they find. You should have plenty of toys for your dog to play with and you may want to consider crate training, for when you are not at home. Crate training should begin right after you bring the dog home. This means the dog will stay in a crate when you go out and will not destroy your home. By placing a blanket, toys and water into the crate, you will make the dog comfortable while you are away.

You should not use the crate when punishing the dog or it will not want to go in it when you leave for the day. After training the dog, you will have to keep up the routine. This will give the dog structure and will also save your possessions. Keeping the dog in a crate when you are not at home will also reduce allergens.

Since the Portuguese Water Dog is not bred as often as other breeds of hypoallergenic dogs, you will have to search for a breeder online, in the newspaper, or by calling breeders in your area until you find one.

While most Portuguese Water Dogs are black, some are white or a mix of both. Their hair is curly or wavy and similar to that of the standard poodle. They need to be groomed every two months or so.

There are two patterns that groomers usually create, the retriever cut and the lion cut. The retriever cut means that the hair is cut evenly on the body. The lion cut leaves the front half of the dog's body covered with hair, while the fur on the hind legs is cut short.

Portuguese Water Dogs typically live between twelve and fifteen years.

Tesco Pet Insurance   **Glossary**

C—H

Conjunctivitis - a bacterial or viral eye infection that causes a sticky discharge and irritation.

Cysts - blocked sebaceous glands on the skin's surface.

Ecto-parasiticide - a strong insecticidal formula used for external parasites.

Electro-magnetic - relating to the interrelation of electric currents or fields and magnetic fields.

Elizabethan collar - a plastic cone-shaped ruff worn round the neck that prevents the cat nibbling or licking any part of their body or paws.

Entire female - a cat that hasn't been spayed and is, therefore, capable of becoming pregnant and having kittens.

Gingivitis - gum disease characterised by reddened or bleeding gums at the base of the teeth.

Haemoglobin - cells that carry oxygen around the body.

Haemorrhage - an internal bleed.

Halti - a head collar for dogs that tend to pull on a normal lead and choke themselves.

Thread 4: Finding Hypoallergenic Dog Breeders

Before you visit a dog breeder, you will have to conduct a little research into the type of dog you are looking for. Some breeders, unfortunately, might take advantage of you, if you appear as if you don't know much about dogs. They might try to sell you a mixed breed, or a dog that is sick, or a dog that is not hypoallergenic. Finding a good dog breeder when you want to buy a hypoallergenic dog will be a problem, if you do not know what you are looking for.

One way to learn about the breed of hypoallergenic dog you might want to bring into your home is to visit the library or the internet. You can look for information about specific breeds that are considered to be hypoallergenic and also about their dispositions, types of living conditions best fitted for them, and how to care for a dog once you bring it home. You can also see pictures of the dogs. This will help you when you visit a breeder. Your research should also include information about the price typically paid for specific breeds.

In addition, often breeders advertise on the internet, at veterinarian offices, in the newspaper, and on community bulletin boards.

After you have decided which breed of dog you would like, research breeders in your area. You should find out if breeders are licensed before you pay them a visit. You can learn this information simply by calling the breeder or calling local or national breeding agencies. They will be able to tell you if the breeder is licensed, which types of hypoallergenic dogs he breeds, and if he has any complaints filed against him.

If you think you have found a legitimate dog breeder, then you should visit him to see which breeds he has available. You should take note of the condition the dogs are kept in, ask the ages of the dogs; and when you are looking at specific dogs, you should see if their skins, eyes, and coats look healthy. Even though this will only tell you so much, it may be enough for you to decide if the dog is healthy enough to take home.

How much you should pay for your new dog will depend on the breed. Hypoallergenic dogs usually cost more than other breeds, but if you have allergies, you might not have a choice.

Most pure bred dogs can cost a few hundred dollars. Breeders do not usually offer a return policy, so make sure that you buy the breed you want. If the price seems too high or too low, check with other breeders in the area. Do not buy from the breeder if you suspect you are not getting the dog you asked for.

Take the dog to your vet to make sure the dog is healthy soon after bringing it home.

Buying a new dog is not always easy, but if you are careful about whom you do business with, you will find the perfect dog for your lifestyle.

Tesco Pet Insurance   **Glossary**
H—L

Harness - designed to fit around the dog's body and legs, attaching on the back, in between the shoulder-blades. Designed to stop a dog pulling harshly on his lead.
Haunches - hind quarters/legs.
Hock - the joint in a dog's hind leg between the knee and the fetlock, the angle of which points backwards
Hypersensitivities - extreme physical sen- sitivities to particular substances or conditions. **Hypoallergenic** - relatively unlikely to cause an allergic reaction.
Infectious canine hepatitis - a liver disease that a dog can pass on in his urine for up to six months after being cured.
Inguinal - affecting the groin.
Insecticides - chemical substances used for killing insects.
Ke tones - substances made when the body breaks down fat or energy.
Kong - a cone-shaped hard rubber toy which has spaces to insert treats.
Larynx - voice box.
Leptospirosis - carried by rats and foxes and passed from dog to dog in infected urine.

Thread 5: How to Care for Hypoallergenic Dogs

Hypoallergenic dogs are sold by breeders, but you can also find them in pet stores and sometimes in animal shelters. If you decide to buy a hypoallergenic dog, there are certain ways to care for him that may require a bit more work than you had imagine.

Caring for your hypoallergenic dog begins with caring for his coat. While many hypoallergenic breeds such as Terriers, Schnauzers, and Poodles have short hair, this hair can be coarse and will continue to grow unless the dogs are properly groomed. These dogs do not shed and have hair that can be compared to human hair. You will have to keep your dog groomed in order to prevent matting. Matting can cause skin rashes and other health problems.

Brushing your dog is also important especially for breeds that have longer hair such as the Afghan Hound. While these dogs are considered hypoallergenic, their coats are long and shiny. They do not shed either, so brushing and grooming are important. Brush your dog at least twice a week to keep excess hair from building up. As mentioned earlier, some hypoallergenic dogs have undercoats, while others do not. Undercoats protect dogs from cold temperatures by storing body heat. Dogs that don't have undercoats will not survive long in cold temperatures. Unless the breeder says you can keep your dog outside, you should keep your dog indoors.

If you have a hairless dog, you will have to protect its skin with lotions and skin creams. You should not leave these dogs outside for long periods of time as they will suffer from sun burn and dehydration. Protecting your hypoallergenic dog from cold temperatures, the sun, and from developing skin rashes are ways that you can help your dog live a long, healthy life.

Caring for your dog is not only making sure his coat and skin are protected; it also means making sure that he gets enough exercise and quality time with you each day. Dogs left alone for long periods of time can become destructive. Training your dog by developing a routine will help him adjust to the times when you cannot be at home. If you will be out of town for more than two or three days, you should find a friend that can check in on your dog or you should consider boarding the dog until you come home.

Because many breeds of hypoallergenic dogs are small in size, they are prone to arthritis, eyesight issues, tumors, and other problems. While you cannot predict how your dog will age, you should research different breeds to see what types of health issues they may have some day. Regular checkups with a vet will help your dog live a long life.

Tesco Pet Insurance **Glossary**

M—P

Metaldehyde - a form of insecticide used to kill slugs.

Microchip - a tiny device that's injected in the scruff of the neck and holds personal information about the pet permanently. **Neutered** - a cat or dog that's had an operation to make it sterile i.e. unable to make a female pregnant or to have kittens, if female.

Neutering - a routine operation to stop a dog or cat being able to make a female pregnant or to stop a bitch from ever conceiving puppies. Male dogs are castrated, that is, they have their testes removed while a bitch will have the uterus and ovaries removed.

Ophthalmic - concerned with the eye and treatment of the disorders that affect it.

Otitis externa - outer ear canal.

Over-bite - in a dog, the teeth should mesh together when the animal bites but if the upper or lower jaw juts out further, this is an under- bite or an over-bite.

Periodontal - concerning the structures that support the teeth.

Pharynx - throat.

Thread 6: Grooming and Brushing Tips for Dogs That Are Hypoallergenic

Grooming is an essential part of taking care of a hypoallergenic dog. If you do not have the time to schedule regular appointments, then you might have to schedule three of four grooming sessions a year. Most hypoallergenic breeds have short coats that resemble human hair rather than traditional fur. As a result, these dogs shed as much as humans, which means they require regular haircuts just as human beings do.

While there are tools you can use to groom your dog, if you do not feel comfortable or if your dog gets angry when you try to groom it, then you will have to find a professional groomer to trim your dog's hair.

Groomers can be found in the phone book, online, or at chain pet stores. Finding a groomer is not difficult, but possibly finding one that does a good job can be.

The first time your dog visits a groomer, tell the groomer how much hair to trim. When you bring the dog home, inspect the hair to see that the cut is even, that there are no cuts on the dog's skin, and that the hair was cut to your specifications. If the groomer did not do his job, then you should find a new one. But if the dog was happy being with the groomer and the groomer did what you asked, then you should continue visiting him.

Groomers can also trim the hair on your dog's face and clip their nails.

In between grooming sessions, you will have to brush your dog so that the hair does not clump or become matted to its skin. Matting can cause a lot of health issues and could cause the dog discomfort. A good grooming brush won't cost too much and your groomer can recommend the right style for your dog.

Always brush in the direction of the hair and not against it, because this will cause matting to occur. Your dog should enjoy the way the brushing feels. You can brush your dog at any time as long as he feels comfortable. It will only take a few minutes to properly brush your dog.

Matted hair can be difficult to untangle and you may have to bathe your dog in order to loosen the knots. Do not pull too hard or your dog will get upset. If the matted piece will not untangle, you should wait until the next grooming session for it to be cut out. If knots persist, then you might have to brush your dog more often or have its hair cut even shorter.

Grooming and brushing are two ways that pet owners can show love toward their pets. Hypoallergenic dogs are special because more people can tolerate being around them. In return, it is your job to make sure their coat is always healthy.

Tesco Pet Insurance   **Glossary**

P—T

Plaque - a rough, sticky coating on the teeth that consists of saliva, bacteria and food debris, usually found at the margins of teeth and gums.

Puppy crate - a self-contained pet cage with a wipe-clean base that can be used as a safe sleeping area for your puppy.

Rex - the coat has a thick velvety feel due to the structure of the hairs being bred differently.

Satin - the coat has a rich, satin sheen and is due to selective breeding changing the structure of the coat.

Tartar - a hard, deposit
crust-like deposit found on the crowns and roots of teeth, formed when mineral salts from saliva are deposited in existing plaque.

Toxoplasmosis - a parasitic infection in cats that can be passed on via their faeces if left unwormed.

Training pad - an absorbent, waterproof- backed sheet that can be laid on the floor for your dog to wee on and thrown away after use. Available through pet stores and some vets.

Thread 7: Special Needs of Hypoallergenic Dogs

Hypoallergenic dog breeds have special needs because they are usually smaller in size and have temperaments that may be difficult to handle sometimes. When you first bring your new dog home, you should allow it to roam around to get an idea of its surroundings. If you have other pets, you should put them in another room while the dog is investigating the area. Depending on the breed of dog, he may be very scared at first. He may not want much human contact, so you should be careful about handling him too much during the first few days he is in your home.

Once you new dog becomes comfortable, you should develop a feeding and hair brushing routine that you and your dog will follow. If you have allergies, brushing your dog every day will reduce the amount of allergens in the air. This will reduce the allergens on your carpets, furniture, clothing, and walls. Buy a steel comb with wide teeth that will help trap hair and get out any knots that may be in the dog's fur. If you purchased a Mexican hairless or other breed that does not have hair, you should make sure that its skin is not dry.

If you notice flaking, you should visit your vet who will prescribe medication or a lotion you can use.

Making sure your hypoallergenic dog gets plenty of exercise is important for his health and also important for controlling allergens in your home.

Walking your dog at least once a day and making sure it sleeps through the night will keep the dog on a routine. Dogs that are awake at night time may want to be with you. Allowing your dog to sleep on your bed, however, could increase your risk of an allergy attack.

Your dog should have a designated place to sleep during the night and during the day. Buying a soft bed or giving the dog an old blanket will help keep him warm and safe when he is sleeping. You should wash his pet bed often to prevent allergens from being transferred to carpeting or clothing. While you cannot prevent all allergens from getting into your clothing and inside your carpeting, you can reduce them by keeping everything in your home clean.

Dog grooming is also important when caring for a hypoallergenic dog. Even though the breed that you buy will probably have short hair, you will have to have it professionally groomed every few months to maintain the shape and also to keep the hair from becoming too long. Since hair can grow long and cover the dog's eyes, and make it difficult for the dog to keep itself clean, grooming your dog will ensure that it remains healthy and happy.

Now that you know something about caring for a hypoallergenic dog, remember that just because the dog is considered a good choice for people with allergies, this doesn't mean he can't cause allergy attacks from time to time. Hypoallergenic dogs reduce the risk of attacks, but don't prevent attacks from occurring.

Tesco Pet Insurance   **Glossary**

U—V

Umbilical - the navel.
Urethra - the tube that carries urine out of the body from the bladder.
Warfarin - used as rat poison, causes massive internal bleeding.

Thread 8: Caring for Dogs with Hypoallergenic Reactions

All dogs have the potential to be allergic to something. Some dog breeds are more susceptible to allergies than others. This may be because of small nasal passages, allergic reactions to flea bites, irritable stomachs that make digesting food difficult, or the dogs may be allergic to their own hair and dander. Dogs that have allergies include the following breeds: Bishon frise, terrier, retrievers, beagles, setters, and boxers.

The most common signs of allergies include raw skin where the dog has scratched, patches of hair missing, red skin, hives, coughing, sneezing, excessive chewing and licking of paws, watery eyes, vomiting, and diarrhea. Sometimes changing the type of dog food or buying a flea collar or spray is enough to help eliminate your dog's allergy problems. While these symptoms may go away after a few days, you should monitor the dog's behavior to see if the symptoms return. If they do, then take the dog to a vet.

When a dog is suffering from allergies, his mood or disposition might change. He might become irritable, lethargic, clingy, or angry. Discipline will not work when a dog is having allergy issues. The best way to combat this problem is to learn how to care for your dog once you have established the cause of the allergies. This means keeping a journal or photos (or video) of the dog's activities and symptoms. You can show these to the vet, who will recommend treatment.

Some smaller breeds have breathing issues as they age. There is little that can be done except to keep their sleeping area clean, vacuum often, and consider buying a hepa diffuser or furnace filter that will trap dust, particles, and other air pollutants in the air.

While it is important that all dogs get exercise, when it is cold outside, keep smaller breeds indoors. This will keep them from getting head colds, which could make breathing worse.

If you notice that your dog has fleas or that he has been bitten by fleas, you should bathe your dog using a shampoo, which will kill fleas and flea eggs. You might have to rid your home of fleas, as well, so that re-infestation does not occur. Buy carpet spray or if the problem is too big, call an exterminator. Once the fleas are gone, you can spray your dog every time the dog goes outside. This will prevent new attacks from occurring. If the dog has open bites or wounds from scratching, however, you will have to wait for the wounds to heal before using a spray or shampoo on your dog.

Vomiting can occur if your dog is allergic to the food it receives. You should first visit the vet to see if the problem isn't internal. The vet may recommend a new food for the dog, which should stop the vomiting and diarrhea. Your vet might prescribe an anti-histamine if the allergies persist.

Dogs that are allergic to their own hair and dander have the worst allergies of all because there is little that can be done. You should make sure your dog is groomed regularly, brush him everyday to remove excess hair and dander, play with him often and bathe your dog once a month.

Thriftyfun   # Dog Glossary

The **Terrier Group** is made up of energetic breeds that are characterized by their bold, feisty and inquisitive nature. Dogs in this group were originally bred for hunting and killing rodents and small game and today are kept primarily as companions. Although they range in size, terriers typically have a distinctively bold and engaging personality. Many have wiry coats that may require special grooming (stripping) in order to main- tain their classic appearance. Terriers can be a bit scrappy and less tolerant of other animals (including dogs), but also make very lively and personable companions.

Thread 9: Dog Health Insurance for Your Pet

The word insurance is one of those words that might make you cringe. You need to keep insurance on your car (it would have been really nice, wouldn't it, if somebody had told you how big a financial drain that likely would be?). Next to putting gas in your car it might seem like the biggest expense you have. If you own a home you probably pay homeowners insurance; if you rent an apartment you probably have renters insurance. What is more, you find yourself struggling with the ever-soaring cost of health care insurance, and if you are truly responsible, you probably have life insurance. But health insurance for your pet? Is that wise?

You love your dog, he's more then a pet, he's a valued member of your family and probably your best friend. And now you find you are hearing that you should consider purchasing a health insurance plan for your pet dog, too. You can barely afford to put food on your table, how are you supposed to be able to afford to insure your pet? Besides he's just a mutt and dog health care insurance is for fancy pure-bred show dogs, not your rescue pet, surely?

If you are living on a shoestring, then that might be the very reason you may want to consider pet health insurance. The average dog owner takes his pet dog to the veterinarian approximately 2-3 times a year and it will cost him approximately two hundred and eleven dollars per year. What happens if your dog contracts a disease, or gets hurt? It doesn't take much to rack up some pretty serious vet bills. You already know how much you have to pay for your own health prescriptions, do you really think that a dog prescription is going to be any cheaper?

Your dog is your best friend and a treasured member of your family but could you live with yourself if you had to put him to sleep, because you couldn't afford his vet bill?

While it might not cover all of your dogs vet care needs, it is possible to get health care insurance for your dog for approximately as low as ten dollars a month. If you shop around and read each plan carefully you might find a pet healthcare plan that will help cover the costs of your pet's routine vet visits.

What if you have to leave town and can't take your dog with you? Can you really afford to leave your dog at a boarding kennel? Some pet insurance plans will even cover a portion of boarding expenses.

Some questions you should ask are whether or not your vet accepts a particular type of insurance, if there is a cap on treatments, how much is your deductible, and how will they handle any pre-existing conditions your dog might have.

Thriftyfun # Dog Glossary

Dog breeds in the **Hound Group** were all originally bred for hunting and pursuing game. This group contains the fastest members of the canine family, like the elegant Greyhound and the Afghan Hound (also known as sight hounds), which are known for their stamina and speed. The group also contains the two tallest dog breeds, the Scottish Deerhound and Irish Wolfhound. Other hounds, such as Rhodesian Ridgebacks, Beagles and Basset Hounds are known for their keen scenting ability and and their stamina in the field.

Thread 10: A Comparison of Five Pet Health Insurance Plans

Currently there are only a handful of companies that offer pet health insurance. Five of the most popular companies are Pets Best Pet Insurance, Veterinary Pet Insurance, ShelterCare, Pets Health and PetCare.

When you are comparing the quote of one health insurance company to another, remember that the base dollar amount is not the only number you have to consider. In addition to the monthly payment, check out exactly what types of veterinary care and treatments are covered (some basic insurance plans do not include cancer treatment, for instance), check out what kind of deductible you, the pet owner, will be expected to pay, check out if there is a yearly cap on medical expenses, and check out what type of discounts are available.

An insurance plan through Pets Best Pet Insurance will cost approximately $32.00 a month ($384.00 annually). Pets Best will cover pet sterilization provided the pet owner purchases an additional wellness plan. Pets Best does not cover pre-existing medical conditions a pet may have so its best to insure a pet early in life before problems develop. Pets Best has a life time limit of $99,750 dollars per pet. Pets Best health insurance plans come with a $75.00 deductible. Multiple pet discounts are available. Pets Best's pet health insurance does cover cancer.

Veterinary Pet Insurance is a company that offers pet owner a $14,000 a year cap on an insurance plan that only costs approximately $20.00 dollars a month. Veterinary Pet Insurance offers plans with a $50.00 deductible (after the deductible they pay ninety percent of the bill) on plans that include pet sterilization and cancer coverage. Veterinary Pet Insurance does not accept pre-existing conditions and does not offer multi-pet discounts.

ShelterCare is a pet insurance that costs pet owners approximately $29.95. For that $29.95 there is absolutely no deductible and cancer treatments are covered. ShelterCare will not pay for pet sterilization nor will they cover any pre-existing conditions. ShelterCare does not have a benefit cap. ShelterCare offers premium discounts for multi-pet plans, medical service, and microchips.

A pet health insurance policy through PetsHealth insurance company will cost the pet owner approximately $37.17 dollars per month. PetsHealth covers 80% of the pets vet bill after the $100.00 doller deductible is paid. PetsHealth has a $13,000 doller cap per year. PetsHealth does insure pre-existing conditions after ninety days. Multi-pet discounts are available through PetsHealth. PetsHealth does offer pet health insurance plans that cover cancer on a case by case basis.

PetCare is a pet health insurance company that estimates the average cost for a policy for a pet is $29.95 a month. This plan includes a fifty doller deductible. While PetCare is happy to cover the cost your pet's cancer treatments they will not pay for any pre-existing conditions nor will they pay for pet sterilization. PetCare offers discounts for multi-pet plans and medical service.

None of the estimated monthly prices for these insurance companies include any extra insurance riders.

Any one or all of these companies can change their policies between now and the time you purchase a pet health insurance plan.

Remember to read the fine print before you sign up for a pet health insurance plan.

All five of these pet health insurance companies have their own websites where you can find up to date pet health insurance quotes. There are other pet health insurance companies with different prices, discounts, stipulations, and benefit caps if you are not satisfied with the above five comparisons.

Thread 11: AKC Pet Health Insurance

As a pet owner, you might either love them or hate them. They are the members, breeders, and owners who are affiliated with the American Kennel Club. The American Kennel Club is the largest registry of pure bred dogs in the entire world.

Puppies who are registered with the American Kennel Club are the aristocracy of the dog world, granted entry into the finest clubs and most exclusive clubs. Dogs of breeds not recognized by the American Kennel Club or dogs that are of a mixed ancestry can make their owners feel embarrassed.

For all the hoopla surrounding the American Kennel Club only its members seem to actually know what it really is. The American Kennel Club has been registering puppies for over one hundred and twenty-two years. In 2006 there were over nine hundred thousand dogs registered with the American Kennel Club. In 2006 the AKC signed a contract with the pet stores Petland but later rescinded the offer after a flurry of controversy.

In addition to registering dogs the American Kennel Club also hosts several large shows including the Westminster Kennel Club Dog Show (it is actually older then the kennel club) and the AKC/Eukanuba National Championships.

In addition to hosting dog shows and overseeing the registration of hundreds of thousands of dogs each year the American Kennel Club also takes an active interest in canine health research. Some dog owners are familiar with their current advertising campaign promoting their commitment to healthy dogs.

Because the American Kennel Club realizes that the high cost of veterinary care can be difficult for many dog owners to afford they now offer AKC pet health insurance. The American Kennel Club Healthcare Plan is designed to help offset the high cost of Veterinary treatments, surgery, and prescriptions.

On the American Kennel Club website they have a list of claims that have successfully been rewarded to dog owners who purchased an AKC pet health care plan. These claims include a $2,600.00 dollar claim for poison toadstools, and a recent case of bee stings for which they paid a claim of $2,200, and a claim for which the owners of a dog bitten by a snake received a check for $1,262, and $2,000 for a claim of an intestinal resection, and $2,800 paid out for a ruptured ligament. The biggest claim currently listed on the website is for a ruptured vertebral disc that would have cost the owners an additional $3,329 out of their own pockets.

The American Kennel Club estimates that the average daily cost of a healthcare plan for your dog is approximately sixty-eight cents a day (this is based on the Essential plan's annual price). You can pick from four different types of healthcare insurance plans, you have a variety of wellness options you can choose that will help cover dental cleaning, shots, and checkup.

Applying for the insurance is supposed to be easy and you can choose to pay monthly or yearly. You get to continue to use you very own veterinarian. The American Kennel Club also offers coverage for cats.

One of the really nice features about the AKC pet healthcare coverage is the sixty-day complimentary trial period.

Thriftyfun   **Dog Glossary**

The **Herding Group** was created by the American Kennel Club in 1983 to recognize members of the working group that excel at herding and controlling the movement of other animals. Many of these breeds are no longer used for herding and are more often kept as household pets. They are intelligent and easy to train, and many kept as companions still retain strong instincts to herd-even trying to gently herd their owners or the children in the family. Examples of herding breeds include Old English Sheepdogs, Corgis, Collies, Australian Cattle Dogs and the Puli.

Thread 12: Animal Health Insurance for your pet Ferret

Ferrets are long, silky, fun filled, and cuddly. They can provide endless hours of fun. They can also give you a migraine as you try to pay for the vet bills you didn't think about when you spontaneously purchased that impossibly cute ferret, with the incredibly pointed face, from your local pet store. The first thing you might learn about your pet ferret is that not only will it love to have your undivided attention, it can also catch that twenty-four hour flu you had a few days ago.

The ability to catch diseases from their human owners is one of those unique traits that separates ferrets from cats and dogs (cats and dogs cannot catch the flu from humans). Hopefully now that you are armed with this knowledge you will be savvy enough to bring your pet ferret to the veterinarian (preferably one with knowledge and experience about ferrets) before it starts showing flu-like symptoms. Ferrets are very sturdy animals when healthy but once they get sick they can go downhill fast. It is important your veterinarian sees your pet and prescribe a treatment as soon as possible

Young ferrets are often fed on hard food or pellets before they are really mature enough to manage it. The hard food can cause your new pet to develop a prolapsed rectum (i.e., when the rectum lies outside of the body instead of inside).

Oddly enough this is not normally something

your veterinarian even needs to see. Normally the rectum returns to its normal position after a few days.

Smear a small amount of Preparation-H on the exposed rectum to help keep it moist and keep a close eye on it. Remember that pink is good. As long as the flesh of the prolapsed rectum is a nice healthy- looking rosy pink, it's healthy. If the healthy pink color starts to fade take your pet ferret for a consultation with the vet.

It is important to know your pet's personality, the better you know your ferret's personality the quicker you will be able to recognize any health issues your **ferret** might have. Ferrets suffer from a variety of diseases and tumors such as insulinorma, tumors, heart disease, intestinal conditions, and complications involving the liver and intestines and spleen. Many pet ferrets are plagued with multiple issues at the same time. Most diseases commonly found in ferrets will need some type of veterinary care which will often include surgery.

The average lifespan is 7-10 years old with each year equaling ten human years. The temperature of a healthy ferret is between 100 and 104 degrees, with most of them hovering at a comfortable 101.9 degrees. The heart rate of the average ferret is about 225 beats per minute but it can range from 180-250 beats per minute. Ferrets have an average respiration rate of 33-36 breaths per minute.

If you are concerned about being flooded with

an endless amount of expensive veterinarian bills and don't know if you will be able to pay them, you might consider purchasing animal health insurance for your pet ferret.

Thriftyfun   **Dog Glossary**

The **Toy Group** dog breeds are characterized by their small size and gentle natures. Dogs in the toy group make good companions, especially for people who live in small apartments or houses in the city because they generally require less exercise and living space. These breeds are usually affectionate, alert and loyal, and often make good watchdogs and travel companions. Examples of breeds in the toy group include Chihuahuas, Pomeranians, Papillions, Pekingese and Shih Tzu.

Thread 13: Canada's Pet Health Concerns that Benefit from Canadian Pet Health Insurance

Cancer and Tularemia. These are two health care issues that might make pet owners consider purchasing (Canadian) Pet Health Insurance for their family pets. Cancer is a type of malignant tumor or growth that invades the surrounding tissues and uses the bloodstream to move and spread to other parts of the body. Some cancers reappear even after removal of the offending tumor. Cancer can regenerate unless the tumor is removed and any remaining cancer cells properly treated.

Thanks to improvements in veterinary care and knowledge of nutritional needs, family pets are living longer. As a direct result of the longer life span of pets, more cases of cancer are being recorded.

Signs that the family pet might have cancer are abnormal swellings that continue to grow, sores that don't heal, bleeding or other types of discharge from body openings, a difficult time eating and swallowing, persistent lameness, difficulty breathing, painful urination, chronic coughing, weight loss, fevers, loss of appetite and lack of stamina. Should your pet experience any of these symptoms, consult with your local veterinarian.

If your pet is diagnosed with cancer discuss treatments with the veterinarian and call your pet health care insurance representative to find out what can be done to extend the life of your pet.

In the past, cancer was considered the kiss of death for a beloved pet. In today's medically advanced world, your pet's outcome and outlook can be more positive. Early detection followed by timely intervention is the most positive treatment for your pet's cancer.

In some cases simple removal of the tumor is all that is required. Some types of cancer might require surgery. Surgery to remove cancer has an excellent success rate today, if the cancer is detected early on. But if your pet has a tumor that can't be treated by surgery, then your veterinarian might suggest radiation, chemical, or biological therapy.

Radiation therapy exposes the malignant cells to a high level of radiation with the hope that the radiation will kill the cancer cells.

Chemical therapy is medication design to kill the cancer cells. In particularly aggressive forms of cancer, chemical and radiation therapy may be used jointly.

Other forms of therapies used to treat and comfort your pet (diagnosed with cancer) are grooming, nutritional support, soft bedding, pain management, ulcer prevention, and physical therapy.

Tularemia is caused by a bacterial disease that is most commonly seen in **wild rodents and rabbits**. On October 2, 2004, Health Canada issued an advisory about Tularemia, a potential health concern for **dwarf and regular hamsters**. Although it only happens rarely Tularemia is transferable to humans causing flu- like symptoms.

Tularemia is typically found in all **muskrats, squirrels, beavers, rabbit, skunks, dear, bison, foxes, opossums, and woodchucks**. Although Tularemia is seldom seen in dogs and cats, it can contaminate water, it can infect rabbits through their food, and animals can also be infected by being bitten by contaminated ticks.

The typical symptoms of Tularemia are fever, a loss of appetite, weakness, and diarrhea. If the condition is left untreated, the infected animal frequently dies.

The typical treatment plan for pets infected with Tularemia is to firstly eliminate any infected ticks from your pet's fur. After that, the drugs Strptomycin and Gentamycin are administered from one to two weeks. Tetracycline and Chloramphencicol have also been used to treat pets diagnosed with Tularemia.

Thread 14: Care and Health Insurance for the Asian, Pet Pot-Bellied Pig

Black Beauty became every young girl's dream horse, after his memoirs were so cleverly published. There have also been great books about dogs: such as *Old Yeller* and *Where the Red Fern Grows.* And, recently, a string of mystery novels, featuring sleuthing cats, have earned felines a place in the literary annals. But isn't it curious that some of the animal characters people most remember are pigs? When book lovers think of pigs they either smile, remembering *Pigling Bland* or the sweet innocence of Wilbur as he strutted around the barnyard in *Charlotte's Web* or else shudder with delicious distaste, thinking about how George Orwell's Napoleon ruled the farm, after overthrowing the humans in *Animal Farm*.

Recently pigs have been finding their way into more and more homes as family pets. Many pet owners are delighted by the pig's keen intelligence and dynamic personality. Or they walk into a neat, tidy barn and spot an entire litter of new piglets sleeping in a little pig heap on a bed of straw. The next thing they know they have purchased a young pot-bellied pig and are taking it home.

The first mistake people often make is assuming that a pot-bellied pig would make a good pet for their family. They don't really understand that the cuteness fades...fast. One minute they are holding a cute little piglet, the next they are looking at a short-legged, growing piglet with a strangely shaped skull, drooping jowls, and stiff hair.

The next mistake pet owners make when they purchase a pot-bellied pig is that they assume it will stay miniature-size forever. While it is true that the pot-bellied pig is considerably smaller than its barnyard cousins, pet owners need to understand that the pigs that are used for bacon and Easter hams are normally butchered at weight surpassing three hundred and fifty pounds. The full grown sows can weigh in at well over five hundred pounds.

Once one has purchased a **newborn, pot- bellied pig** you need to start thinking about its health. Pot-bellied pigs need to be spayed or neutered, they need to have their feet trimmed on a regular basis, they need to have their long tusks trimmed, and they need yearly vaccinations.

If you are unable to find a pet health insurance company who is selling coverage for pot-bellied pigs try to get a deal through an insurance company that insures farmers' valuable livestock. Purchasing a pet health plan for your new pet might help make veterinary care more affordable.

If you decide to purchase a health insurance plan for your pot-bellied pig make sure it is one that will still be valid at the end of your pet's life, which could be twenty years away.

In addition to health insurance, pot-bellied-pig owners should probably consider getting some type of liability insurance in case their pot bellied pig accidentally hurts someone. For the most part, pot-bellied pigs are low-key and amiable, but once in a while you can stumble across one that gets irritated with people. Just like their larger, barnyard cousins, pot-bellied pigs are very strong. They can literally toss a full grown man to the side with just a little nudge of their snout.

Thriftyfun   **Dog Glossary**

Dogs in the **Working Group** are often trained for a variety of tasks, including pulling sleds, guarding property and livestock, and performing water and mountain rescues. These breeds are recognized for their intelligence, ability to learn quickly and their alert temperaments. Breeds in this group tend to be strong and larger in size and may not be suitable as pets for the typical family, although they make good companions when properly trained. Great Danes, Si- berian Huskies, Doberman Pinchers

Thread 15: Comparison with Pet Health Insurance in Europe

In Europe over twenty-five percent of all pet owners carry a pet health insurance policy on their pets. Approximately half of Sweden's pet owners carry insurance. A recent poll of pet owners in the United States predicted that only three percent had purchased a pet health care plan.

Many veterinarians feel that three percent is a very generous estimate. One of the big reasons veterinarians believe so many Europeans carry pet health insurance is because of a legislative bill passed in 1971 that stated if a dog was considered at fault for an accident, like a car wreck, then the pet's owner would be held responsible. This prompted many dog owners to purchase something called Third Party Liability Insurance which would pay for any damages caused by the policy holder's pet dog.

Chances are good that if you were to ask ten neighbors how they feel about pet health insurance you would probably hear ten, diverse answers. Some pet owners are fanatical about their pets. They will except nothing but the best for their family pet, the best food, the best water, the best doggie bed, and of course the best medical treatments available. Everytime it even looks like their cat or dog is about to cough or sneeze they rush the pet to the veterinarian's clinic and start a fresh round of antibiotics. Because maintaining the absolute best health care available is quite expensive this type of owner is quick to purchase animal health insurance that promotes good pet medicine. At the slightest hint you might be considering purchasing pet health insurance for your pet, this over-the-top pet owner starts shoving all sorts of flyers and brochures and applications into your hand, sometimes he will even offer to call his pet health insurance representative for you. This would be fine and dandy except that their monthly pet insurance bills are higher then you can afford.

Another owner might love his family pet just as much as the over-the-top owner. He might wish he could provide his pet with the very best but it simply isn't economically possible. This pet owner's advice might be: "Put the money you might have spent on a monthly insurance premium aside and use that to cover your pets medical needs. After all if you put aside thirty dollars a month then you'll have enough money to cover the routine visits to the vet's office plus have a little extra set aside if an emergency happens down the road."

This type of insurance is called self insurance. While it sounds like a good idea there are a couple of problems. Problem one: a medical emergency might happen right away and you might not have saved enough money to cover treatment. You might be forced to accept economic euthanasia for your pet.

A second problem with self insurance is that it's money just "laying around." It's awfully easy to regard it as spare cash and use it on the family vacation or use it as a down payment on that laptop you've always wanted.

If as a pet owner you decide that pet health insurance simply isn't for you, then you will want to check and see if your homeowners insurance covers any potential accidents caused by your pet. If a dog or cat bites somebody, the bitten person can sue you and in some cases demand that the pet be euthanized. If your homeowner's insurance does not cover pet mishaps you should possibly give a lot of thought to purchasing pet liability insurance.

Thread 16: Can Feral Cats Be Tamed?

Feral cats are different from stray cats. Stray cats are usually the product of a person's irresponsibility. Irresponsibility could be defined in two ways when it comes to strays: dumping a cat to fend for itself and/or neglecting to spay and neuter a cat. Stray cats can be timid, but are often easily tamed. Feral cats are cats that were probably born to wild parents and are wild themselves. Feral cats have had no human interaction and are very difficult to tame.

Because feral cats are difficult to tame, this makes them undesirable as indoor pets. There are many rescue organizations that are dedicated to the trapping and spaying and neutering of feral cat colonies. Many times, these organizations trap the cats, have them spayed and neutered and then release them back where they were originally found. Then, they dedicate themselves to providing food to these colonies.

Feral cats are everywhere. You can find feral cats in rural or farm areas, abandoned buildings and even parks and alleyways. You might catch a glimpse of them, but chances are that you would not be able to capture them easily. After all, they have not been around humans so any contact would make them shy away from you.

If you have feral cats in your neighborhood, you may wonder whether these animals can be kept as pets. Taming a feral cat can be a difficult proposition simply because they are not accustomed to humans. Depending on the level of their interactions with humans, some cats might be classified as semi-feral, totally feral or even a converted feral cat. Depending on how your cat is classified, this predicts your potential success at socializing it. In addition, it takes a lot of time, love and patience to tame feral cats.

If you find a mature cat that is feral, chances are you will have little success in socializing it. With no human contact at all, these cats are overly independent and would never depend on a human for food or companionship. You might, of course, have better success with a cat that is semi-feral. In this instance, it will have had some human contact. A converted feral cat would probably have a better chance of a normal life as someone's pet. These cats were once domesticated, meaning they probably started life as a pet and were later abandoned. The converted feral cat will more than likely eventually respond to human interactions, love and affection.

If you want to attempt to tame a feral cat, remember that it can be hard work reaching out to the feral cat and getting him to trust you. Your efforts might not pay off for months, especially with older cats. If your attempts are successful, though, the rewards will be well worth it, because a strong bond can develop and loyalty and love is the reward.

If you believe you have the time and the love to tame a feral, there are some things to remember. First, these cats see you as an intruder and are very likely to spit, hiss, bite and claw. This is a normal response as they are defending themselves against a perceived predator – you (!). If they manage to get in a few bites or scratches, you should apply first aid immediately.

After you have successfully trapped a feral cat, your very first step is to get it to the vet for spay or neuter treatment and to check for any diseases it may carry. This is a necessary step and an absolute must if you have other pets in the house. After you have arrived home with your cat, you need to let it adjust to you and the surroundings by giving it a small, safe place to stay. Allow the cat to stay in a small bathroom or laundry room, where it does not feel overwhelmed. You will need to take time every day to spend time with the cat and allow the cat to adjust to you.

Remember, not all feral cats can be socialized; however with love and patience, your time and efforts could be rewarded.

Thread 17: Domestic Cat Breeds

Have you always wanted a cat but have you heard some breeds make better pets than others? Maybe you have always wanted a cat, but do not know anything about them?

There are plenty of ways to learn about cats and what breeds fit your personality. You have a choice of an indoor, outdoor or indoor and outdoor cat. The tough and smart survive in the outdoors. Small cats, however, can be prey for birds and other wildlife and should be kept indoors. Tomcats, a mixed breed, are great at surviving outdoors and they are "mousers." So let's examine a few breeds of cats and then you may be able to choose which one is right for your lifestyle.

Siamese: Siamese can be great pets, especially when raised from infancy. The Siamese cat can be fickle. They often require a lot of attention, when they want to command it. They tend to mew quite a bit and can tear up a home if left alone too long. These are the downsides.

They are often white with brown ears and blue eyes. You may recognize them in Lady and the Tramp? Those two were a little mean and not the typical portrayal of Siamese cats. Siamese are generally very affectionate. They are also one of the most intelligent of the cat species. They tend to be very social, which is why they meow or "talk" a lot. A sign for attention is usually a very vocal meow much like a baby cry. Siamese typically bond to one person very strongly and are territorial or possessive of that person.

Persian: The Persian cat breed is one of the oldest breeds around. They are longhaired cats with beautiful shinny coats. They are very soft and friendly; however, they are prone to health problems such as allergies. The Persian does not always play as much as other breeds, but they do enjoy a bit of fun and play, especially in a social situation. They love to have other cats around to play with as well as have a lap available when they are in need of a nap. Persians are a variety of colors from solid black, white or a mix of white and browns around the face. A popular Persian is the Himalayan.

Manx: The Manx is known for its stubby tail or for its absence of tail. The downside to Manx cats is the lack of tail. Often a Manx can suffer from worms and other parasites due to improper cleaning and not having the protection of a tail. This does not mean you should discount the Manx as a breed. The Manx breed is extremely intelligent and playful. They are a lot like dogs in the play area because they can fetch when you throw toys and bring them back to you. They are very social animals and depend on human care. They don't like to be left alone for too long, so it is wise to have other cats to play with when you are gone during the day. The best home for a Manx is one filled with children.

The Siamese, Persian and the Manx are just three

of the more popular breeds of cats. There are over a dozen cat breeds to choose from and finding the right one to fit your lifestyle is important. Cats are very social and intelligent, but some breeds can be loners. Most often, a cat chooses when the time is right and what type of attention he wants at the time. The phrase "you do not own a cat, it owns you" is very true.

Thriftyfun   **Dog Glossary**

The Non-Sporting Group consists of a diverse number of dogs breeds all with varying personalities and overall appearances. These breeds are generally kept as companions and in some cases, watchdogs, for the home and family. Examples of dog breeds in this group include the Schipperke, Poodle, Lhasa Apso, Chow Chow, Dalmation and French Bulldog.

Thread 18: Caring For Your Diabetic Cat

If your cat has just been diagnosed with diabetes, you might be afraid of what the future holds for your beloved pet. The good news is that cats can live long, healthy lives after being diagnosed with diabetes. The trick is that you, as a pet owner, must be dedicated to caring for your cat during his or her illness. Diabetes is not a death sentence for pets. Here is some information to help you understand what you need to do to help your diabetic cat.

Regular Medical Care: After your cat has been diagnosed with diabetes, it is imperative that you visit your veterinarian on a regular basis. Your cat will need regular checkups to check the blood sugar levels and to make sure that he or she is receiving the right amount of insulin.

When your cat goes in for a check up, the vet will ask that you do not feed your cat twelve hours before the check up. While your cat is at the check up, your veterinarian will draw blood and check blood sugar levels. People who have diabetes are able to check their blood sugar at home. However, this will not usually be possible for cats, unless you buy a glucose monitoring system. You will probably be asked to bring your cat in every three months for this type of check up.

Getting your Cat Insulin: When your cat has diabetes, it is your responsibility to make sure that your cat receives the proper dose of insulin twice a day. The amount of insulin that your cat will need will vary according to your cat's individual condition. Most cats will receive between three and five units of insulin two times per day. It is important that you establish a routine for your cat. Your cat needs to receive insulin 12 hours apart. Most people who have diabetic cats give their cats an insulin shot at the same time every morning and at the same time every evening.

It is not difficult to learn how to give your cat insulin injections. Your veterinarian will walk you through the process, and then you can repeat this at home. Usually your veterinarian will recommend that you give your cat injections between the shoulder blades in the scruff of the neck. With patience and practice, your cat will barely feel the injections. In fact, most diabetic cats know when it is time to get their injection and they may actually remind you by mewing.

Stocking the Right Supplies: It is important that you have the right supplies on hand to help treat your diabetic cat. You will need a vial of insulin as prescribed by your veterinarian, syringes and alcohol swabs. It is always a good idea to order your insulin when you are about halfway empty. It might take a couple days for your veterinarian to order your insulin.

Your veterinarian might also recommend giving your diabetic cat vitamin supplements or a special prescription diet such as Science Diet W/

D. You must be able to see your cat immediately after it receives its injection. It is also a good idea to have the telephone number of your veterinarian always handy and to know the locations of at least two, 24-hour emergency vet clinics, just in case your cat needs help.

Many people who own diabetic cats worry about the costs that this condition incurs. It certainly does cost money to take care of a diabetic cat. A vial of insulin will cost you approximately $85 and will last you about two months. A box of 100 Syringes will cost about $30 and will last 50 days, as you should use a new syringe for each injection. Prescription food will cost you about $40 for a 20-pound bag. However, it is important to remember that your cat is a part of your family. Many pet owners do not hesitate spending this kind of money on their pets.

Patience and Love: Above all when you have a diabetic cat, you need a lot of patience and a lot of love. It is not always easy to care for a sick and ailing cat. However, with the right care, you can expect your diabetic cat to have many more years of happy life.

Thread 19: Cavy Care: Is A Guinea Pig Right For You?

If you are thinking about getting a pet for your home, you might first consider a dog or cat. These animals are perfect for homes if you have the time to dedicate to owning a pet. Dogs and cats need a lot of attention and a lot of space.

Guinea pigs on the other hand are also cute, and they do not require nearly as much space or care. Guinea pigs are great pets for all types of homes. When you get your guinea pig young, you can socialize it. You and your children will enjoy these adorable pets for many years to come.

Guinea pigs, also called cavies, are lovable furry little critters that will bring you a lot of joy. If you are thinking about getting a pet for your home, you might want to consider a guinea pig. Guinea pigs can be a perfect first pet for children because they are easy to care for and more cuddly than a hamster or fish.

Here is some more information to help you determine whether a guinea pig is the right pet for you. Many people love the idea of guinea pigs as first pets for children, because they live a lot longer than hamsters or gerbils. In fact, a well cared for guinea pig can live up to eight or nine years. Once you own a guinea pig, you will be hooked by these cute, sweet natured critters.

Each guinea pig has his or her own personality. Some are more reserved in nature, while others are more outgoing. When you go to buy a guinea pig, it is always a good idea to look at them carefully and choose them for their personalities.

If you are choosing a guinea pig for your child, you want to make sure that your guinea pig can tolerate being held and petted. Guinea pigs are not known to be aggressive nor to bite, but your child will have no fun with a shy guinea pig.

Guinea pigs are social animals, and they enjoy the company of other guinea pigs. If you are planning to get a guinea pig, you might consider getting two guinea pigs at the same time. Male guinea pigs get along quite well with each other, if gotten when they are babies. But two, grown male guinea pigs will fight each other. Two female guinea pigs can also get along well with each other. It is not recommended, however, that you get a male and a female, unless you want to breed guinea pigs.

When looking for guinea pig cages, you need to find one that will allow enough room for movement and play. Guinea pigs like to stay hidden when they sleep, so make sure your cage has a place where they can hide. A plastic or wooden structure inside the cage is always a good idea. You will also want to add some sort of bedding to the bottom of your guinea pig cage for easy cleanup. Cedar chips are not recommended.

You also want to include a large water bottle for your guinea pig. If you have two guinea pigs consider getting two water bottles. Guinea pigs love to drink water, so make sure that you give them plenty of fresh water every day.

Some experts recommend adding vitamin C drops to the water. This works well for some guinea pigs. However, some guinea pigs do not like the taste and will not drink the water. If you do decide to add vitamin C drops to the water, make sure they are staying hydrated throughout the day. If you choose not to include vitamin C drops with the water, you can supplement their diet with fresh fruits and vegetables. Guinea pigs love fresh vegetables and fruits of all kinds. Just make sure that you are not overfeeding your guinea pigs and use fruits and vegetables as treats. As far as food is concerned, you will want to feed your guinea pigs specially-formulated, guinea-pig pellets, available at pet stores. Guinea pigs also needed a daily supply of Timothy hay to help aid in digestion.

Thread 20: Dangerous Dog Treats: What To Know Before You Treat Your Pup.

If you have a dog, then you have a good idea of what your dog likes to nibble on. What pooch doesn't love getting a treat or two, now and then? Dog owners, in turn, love giving their dog treats.

There are so many treats available these days and they come in all different shapes, sizes, colors, and consistencies. For every great dog treat, however there are those on the market that are not so good. These treats can harm your dog by becoming lodged in its throat or intestines. This can cause choking or worse.

If you love treating your canine friend, then you will want to be aware of the treats that can be potentially harmful. Even with treats that are not usually dangerous, you need to supervise your dogs when they eat. Always pay attention to what kind of treat you give your dog in case of a recall.

Greenies: Most dogs really enjoy these treats. They are advertised as a treats that help clean your dog's teeth. However, you need to be aware that "greenies" can cause choking. This is because dogs eat these very quickly, causing large chunks to lodge in the throat. Young puppies should not eat this treat and also not dogs that are prone to "scoffing" food. If your dog eats these treats, be aware of potential vomiting, bloody stools, and difficulty breath- ing. If you notice any of these symptoms after your dog has eaten this treat, seek medical attention.

Rawhide Chews: Whose dog does not love snacking on these chewy treats? Rawhides are good because they clean your dog's teeth and keeps your dog occupied. However, rawhides are dangerous, as well. Some rawhides that originate outside of the United States may actually be preserved with arsenic-based chemicals that will be ingested by your dog when it chews. For this reason, make certain that any rawhide treat you purchase is processed in the United States where this preservative is forbidden. If you cannot tell where a treat originated, then do not buy it! In addition, you will still need to watch your dog when he is munching on rawhides to help prevent his choking. Make sure you buy rawhides that are the right size for your dog, too. A small dog needs the smaller-size, rawhide treats

Chocolate: Chocolate is a terrible thing to allow dogs to eat. Of course, sometimes dogs get into candy and cake without our knowledge. Chocolate is toxic to both dogs and cats, so you need to be aware of your dog sneaking snacks of chocolate nibbles, especially around the holidays. Chocolate contains an ingredient called theobromine. This acts in the canine about the same way caffeine acts in the human. A little will make the dog hyperactive, but a huge dose can prove fatal. If your dog has gotten into chocolate, you need to look for vomiting, shallow breathing, and irregular heartbeat. A visit to the emergency vet might be necessary.

Bones: It seems that it is the right of every dog to be able to crunch on a real bone from time to time. Dogs love bones of all types. However, some bones can be dangerous. Both chicken and turkey bones are especially dangerous because they are brittle. When your dog chews on them, they can easily splinter and cause choking. Some pork and beef bones can also cause the same problem. Veterinarians agree that one of the safest bones you can give your dog is a shinbone. If you must give your dog a bone, make sure you supervise your pooch and if he or she shows signs of bleeding, then you should call your vet immediately for advice.

This is not to say you cannot give your dog an occasional treat. Doing so is part of the fun of owning a dog. You do need to watch your dog and make sure that your dog is safe when snacking.

Thread 21: Fascinating and Novel Pets: The Turtle

Turtles are both fascinating and novel pets for children. Do you remember reading children's books with turtles as the main character? Children adore turtles as pets. They are very interesting creatures and there are many species.

When you decide to have a turtle for a pet, you will need to know the exact species for the proper care. Let us look at some turtle species you can own. There are two types of turtles, the terrestrial and the aquatic. This means the first type of turtle spends more time on the land, while the aquatic turtle needs to have a great deal of water.

Box and mud turtles are terrestrial turtles. They require land to hibernate during the winter and they sun during the day. Most terrestrial turtles need 12 hours of sunlight, which can be provided by a UV lamp.

Turtles are very susceptible to temperature changes often living in 80 degrees during the day and 70 degrees during the night. Terrestrial turtles also need water not only to drink but also to swim in.

Aquatic turtles are either sliders or painted turtles. Sliders typically live in swampy areas or near lakes with a lot of mud. During the day, they tend to bask in the sun as well as swim to cool off. Painted turtles like the sliders are mostly aquatic, so they spend more time in the water than sunning. Painted turtles require special care.

Once you have decided which type of turtle you have you will then have to decide which size tank to use. Most turtles require a 40 gallon tank or larger to have room for land and water.

You will want to have plants in the tank, but make sure they are not poisonous, because your turtle will eat them. Your pet shop should be able to tell you the right type of plants to have.

Certain turtles should have small rocks to burrow under along with the dirt.

Wood chips and bark are not a good idea. Not only do they harbor bacteria and molds, but the turtle can eat them. A turtle does not have a large digestive track and therefore wood chips often cause blockages.

Some proper food for turtles is lettuce, goldfish, special feed sticks, berries and insects depending on the species of turtle you own.

Water is very important to your turtle. You never want to give them tap water to drink. It is best to give them natural spring water or non-chlorinated water for swimming in. Chlorine and other chemicals of tap water can cause bacteria in their digestive systems.

Turtles can make great pets if you know a little about their habitat needs. Turtles are wondrous creatures that you find, in most warm climates, walking along the roads or basking in the sun. So what better pet to give your child than a turtle?

Keep in mind that turtles are sensitive and you

will not want to handle them a lot. They do need to hibernate in order to live a longer life, which requires that you keep the turtles somewhere, where little children cannot disturb them, during the fall period.

Thriftyfun   # Dog Glossary

Breeds in the **Sporting Group** are bred to work closely with people and are characterized by their responsive natures and high degree of intelligence. These dogs are naturally active and alert and known for their instincts and ability in the water and woods. These breeds excel at tracking game, indicating targets and retrieving, and are usually associated with hunting and field work. Examples of dogs that make up the sporting group include Spaniels, Setters, Retrievers, Poodles and Pointers The dogs require lots of regular physical and mental exercise to stay healthy.

Thread 22: Ferrets A Friendly Playful Pet

Ferrets are often considered a rare pet to own. Most individuals choose dogs, cats, birds, or fish to complete their family, however a select few turn to the ferret, because of its sociable, playful and curious qualities. Ferrets love to play and explore not only with others, but also on their own. For this reason, you need to know a little about how to take care of a ferret.

First, you will want to ferret-proof your home before you introduce them as pets. They will crawl into walls, furniture, and anywhere they can get their little bodies. It is much like child-proofing a home for a baby. You will want to make sure all of the dangers are eliminated when you allow them out of their cages for playtime.

Ferrets are also biters. The kits, baby ferrets, tend to bite more. You can eliminate the problem or tone it down with frequent handling. Mock fighting or sparring is typical ferret behavior. The younger ferrets tend to bite more when they are teething and do not mean any harm. For this reason, you will want to handle the ferret or ferrets as often as possible to help reduce the biting behavior. Often those who do not take the time or patience to train their ferret end up leaving the animal in its cage and thus it has a shorter lifespan. Please make sure you are up to the task of training a ferret before bringing one into your home. Trained properly they can be as great a pet as a cat or dog.

A ferret's lifespan is usually six to ten years, however proper care and feeding can lead to a slightly longer lifespan expectancy. Ferrets are carnivores so they require a high protein diet. Most owners decide to feed their ferret's mice, rats, rabbit, and other raw meats such as chicken. Stores carried other types of ferret food that many owners choose over the live food. Carefully reading the label will tell you if it has the proper high protein diet. Most kitten food can be used for example because it is designed to be high protein and fat for growing cats.

While play is an important part of your ferret's life so is sleep. Most ferrets spend fourteen to eighteen hours a day sleeping. Part of sleeping is to rejuvenate them from the active play life they have. They love to explore and to play with toys. Many pet stores have toys for ferrets, or you might have something around the house that your ferret will find appealing.

The type of cage is important. **Ferrets** tend to be very smart so you will need a cage, in which they can get plenty of air, but with small enough bars that they cannot break out. You will also want to clean the cage once or twice a week depending upon the number of ferrets you have or how dirty the cage looks. Ferrets are also burrowers so some type of bedding is required.

Ferrets are little balls of fur that love to play and

interact with humans and each other. While there are some special concessions you need to make to have a ferret, the results are worth it. Proper training of a ferret when a kit will give still more joy as it reaches adulthood.

Dog Glossary

The Chow Chow has an abundant and profuse double coat that comes in two different varieties: smooth or rough. The fur is particularly thick around the neck area and resembles a lion's mane. The outer coat is coarse and is supported by a dense under coat. The most common coat colors are red, black, blue, tan, and gray. They are never parti-colored. The Chow is a heavy seasonal shedder.

The Chow Chow is an ancient breed that originated in China more than 2000 years ago. They were an all purpose breed used for hunting, herding, pulling, and protection. They are commonly referred to as "the Chow", and are now used primarily as a companion.

The Chow Chow is a true masterpiece of dignity and beauty. They possess the unique characteristic of having a blue-black tongue. They are keenly intelligent, have an independent spirit, and display a dignified demeanor. The Chow is extremely aloof and discerning.

The Chow Chow is most generally polite and patient. They are very loyal and friendly with their family, but exceedingly reserved with strangers. They most often will become attached and overly protective of one particular member of the family. They are bossy, serious, and obsti- nate. The Chow Chow is a very dominant breed that requires a dominant owner. They are stubborn and have a mind of their own. They are not good with other pets unless they have been raised with them from an early age. They get along well with older well-behaved children. The Chow expects to be treated with respect.

Thread 23: Hamsters Fuzzy Balls Of Fun

As children, we grew up with hamsters or grew up with friends who had hamsters. Now it is our children, who are probably fascinated with the small fuzzy creatures.

There are many types of hamsters: dwarf, Syrian, Russian, Chinese, and hybrid. The hamster is a burrower so they prefer to have lots of bedding to hide under as well as tubes to create little nests in.

The most difficult aspect of hamsters is telling if they are female or male. Who hasn't bought two hamsters thinking they were the same gender and ended up with ten hamsters?

A lot of biologists and geneticists use hamsters and other rodents to demonstrate genetic principles. In genetics, we often discuss the genome and how genes contribute to eye color, hair color, and other traits. When you have hamsters as pets you can witness this first hand. I had one gold hamster and one white hamster. When they bred I ended up with several color traits from gold, white, black, white and black to others. Half the fun for kids is seeing the baby hamsters grow up with different colors. It can be a great science project for school, too.

Hamsters are relatively easy to take care of. You can feed them hamster food, vegetables, and little hamster treats to give them a good life. The bedding should be changed weekly or twice a week depending upon how many hamsters you have. The downside to hamsters is they have short lives. Most live only a year or two making it difficult on the younger children.

There are lots of hamster accessories from tubes to wheels. Hamsters, like pet mice, need exercise, so giving them wheels to run on or having a hamster ball to run around the house in is good for them. The tubing and cages come in a variety of colors to add to a child's fun. You can create straight pathways to other larger home areas or curve them around to re-enter the same cage. Most of the caging is plastic and your hamster will try to chew or claw his way free. You will want to monitor his activity when you clean the cage to make sure they are not producing a hole. Some hamster owners go with a metal wire cage with tiny slits to avoid the chewing escape. Your preference will determine the type of accessories you purchase. Dwarf hamsters are very susceptible to infections with cedar chips because the chips can tear holes in their tiny mouths.

Handling hamsters should be kept to a minimum and you should always wash your hands, before and after. Hamsters can have a tendency to bite if they are not handled at least once a day or if they become scared. Be cautious with little children.

Hamsters are a lot of fun for all ages whether you have a budding scientist or just want an easy pet your child can care for. You will want to make sure you treat your hamster properly by not overfeeding him and by also maintaining proper exercise. When your hamsters procreate, you will want to separate out the mother and children from the rest of the crew.

Pet Rats

Rats as Pets

"Rats are clean, intelligent, affectionate animals which bond to their human companions in much the same way that dogs do, and with the right care should provide a comparable level of companionship. They are the same species as the wild brown rat, Rattus norvegicus, but have been selectively bred for looks and temperament for at least the last century and are now quite different in tem- perament from their ancestors. They are far less aggressive towards humans and rival rats, and display a number of behavioural differences from wild rats, which have been noted by researchers. Rats become very attached to their owners, make playful, sensitive pets, and can be taught to come by name and learn a variety of tricks. Unlike many other rodents, however, rats are a fairly high maintenance pet. They need at least an hour's playtime outside their cage every day. Because they are much more intelligent than many other small animals, rats can suffer greatly if not given enough attention, free-range time, and environmental stimulation. While rats are extremely rewarding pets and will repay any attention and affection you give them a thousand fold, they may not be suitable for everyone; if you cannot guarantee to give your rats at least an hour of quality time every day, then perhaps a lower maintenance pet would be more suitable."

© A. Robinson & A. Horn 1998-2007, all rights reserved.

Thread 24: Helpful Hermit Crab Basics

Hermit crabs are fun pets to care for in your home. They used to be bought as souvenirs from seaside vacation spots, but now they can be bought almost anywhere. They make wonderful starter pets for kids. They make a great alternative to the more traditional gerbils or hamsters, and they have a much longer life-span than goldfish! Contrary to what you might expect if you are new to hermit crabs, it is possible to play with them, and they do have little personalities of their own. Do you think hermit crabs may make a great pet for you? Here are some helpful hints to get you started.

Before you get your crab, you need to get the basic equipment and supplies in place. First, it will need an aquarium for its house. Forget those teeny, tiny cages you see at the shops by the beach; hermit crabs really need a ten-gallon aquarium to be comfortable. If you are getting more than one crab, obviously you will need a bigger aquarium. A pet shop will be able to advise you on the best size for the number of crabs you will be housing. Make sure the aquarium has a snug fitting lid so your little friends do not make a run for it! Place a heating pad under the tank to keep your crabs feeling nice and tropical.

You will need something to cover the floor of the tank, as well. Three to four inches of sand works best, but you can also use crushed coral or reptile fiber bedding. If you use something other than sand, it is still a good idea to cover a portion of the floor with sand, so the crabs will have somewhere comfortable to go when they molt.

Now that you have the house and the flooring covered, you will need to get two shallow water dishes and a food dish. Shallow shells work well for this job. In one water dish, you should keep fresh water, and in the other, keep salt water, made with a marine aquarium salt solution. The dishes need to be shallow enough for the crabs to crawl into. A natural sea sponge is a nice addition to the fresh water dish, your crab will love to pinch it, and it will help keep the humidity levels up in the aquarium.

The last thing you will need to gussy up your hermit crab home is some decorative wood pieces for the crabs to climb on. Coral and coconut shells also make great additions that your crab will love to play with.

Once you get your crab, to feed it, you will need to get some commercial hermit crab food. You can supplement that food with small pieces of fruit, meat, cereal, or fish. Additionally, make sure your crabs get crushed eggshells or oyster shells to boost their calcium level; it is important to keep their fragile skeletons strong. Cuttlebone is another option for this purpose.

To care for your crabs, clean their water and food

dishes daily, and spot clean the tank when necessary. You will want to provide plenty of extra shells, in increasingly larger sizes, so your crab can change homes as they grow. Shells with wide openings are best. When your crab molts, remove the skin they have shed as soon as possible.

One optional, but useful accessory to get is a tank thermometer and humidity-measuring instrument. Your hermit crab will be most comfortable when the temperature is kept around 72° F - 80°F and the humidity level is between 70% and 80%.

With these helpful hints, you are ready to get your hermit crab. All that is left to do now is come up with a name for your new pet!

Thread 25: Getting Your Pet Via An Animal Rescue Group

Animal rescue organizations or groups offer you a great place to get your next family pet. These groups are all different, but they do have common goals. These groups work hard to locate a permanent loving home for unwanted or misplaced cats and dogs. You will find that most of these groups do rely on their hard working volunteers and support from the local community to operate. They also rely on volunteers and donations to care for these pets while they are between homes.

You will also find a wide variety of animals available through these rescue groups. Many of these groups handle all types of animals and you will find kittens, puppies, and even older pets available for adoption. You might be surprised to learn that some groups even offer exotic pets such as reptiles, pot-bellied pigs and even guinea pigs.

As you begin looking at pets available via rescue groups, keep in mind some of these animals have had very hard lives. You may find a dog that was abused by its owner. You may find a female cat that has just given birth. Their owners have relinquished many of the animals offered to rescue groups, because they are moving or can no longer care for them. In addition, some of these groups take animals that live in kill shelters or strays living on the streets. Some programs also offer spay and neutering programs for feral cats.

Rescue groups do a good job of screening animals before placing them out to new homes. They also screen potential pet owners. If you find a pet offered through a pet rescue group, you will be asked to sign a contract saying you agree to care for the pet long term.

You will also be asked several questions about your home, your children and other pets you may have. This is not to be nosey; it is simply to help match an owner with the right pet. You will probably be asked about other pets you may have, the age of your children, the size of your yard and your thoughts on a cat with claws if you are looking at a cat. This is to help match the pet with the right owner.

If the animal suffers from a medical condition, such as diabetes, the new owners know this up front before adopting. Having the animal's health history at the time of adoption helps the animal find a permanent home.

You can gain a lot of personal satisfaction by adopting your next pet through an animal rescue organization. You know you have done something to help and your new pet will show its appreciation. If you are interested in adopting through one of the many rescue organizations, it is easy to find one in your area. Your vet can give you the contact information for organizations near you. Most of the time, these pets are kept in private homes (foster homes) until they are adopted. This gives the animal time to be socialized with other pets, children, etc. and gives it time to get used to living in a home. Sometimes, animal rescue groups will bring their animals that need homes to pet stores or other locations for interested people to see and meet the animals, say on certain week-ends.

When you choose a pet in a rescue program, be prepared to go through an interview and application process. Adoption fees vary by each organization, but you can expect to pay $100-$200 for a rescued animal. These groups do not make a profit. These fees cover the cost of the animal while it was in the care of the organization. This adoption fee usually covers vaccinations, medical exams, spaying, and neutering. Getting your next pet through an animal rescue organization is a responsible way to get your next family member. You can also find many volunteer opportunities through these organizations

Read

DIARY OF A MOUSE TAMER

http://www.authorstream.com/Presentation/ldlco-2077707-diarymousetamer

www.ingramcontent.com/pod-product-compliance
Lightning Source LLC
Chambersburg PA
CBHW071310040426
42444CB00009B/1952